JENNIFER ARMSTRONG

Spirit of Endurance

Illustrated by William Maughan

Crown Publishers ♛ New York

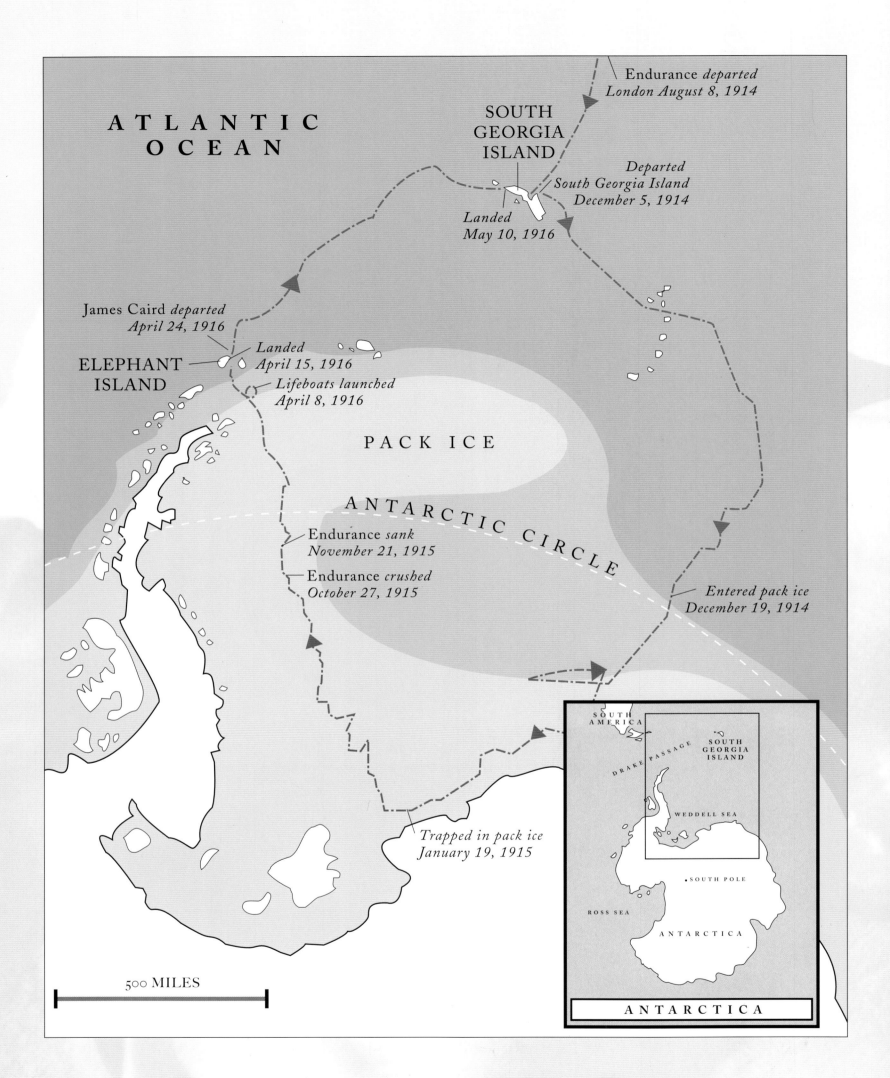

ATLANTIC
OCEAN

SOUTH
GEORGIA
ISLAND

Endurance departed
London August 8, 1914

Departed
South Georgia Island
December 5, 1914

Landed
May 10, 1916

James Caird *departed*
April 24, 1916

Landed
April 15, 1916

ELEPHANT
ISLAND

Lifeboats launched
April 8, 1916

PACK ICE

ANTARCTIC CIRCLE

Endurance sank
November 21, 1915

Endurance crushed
October 27, 1915

Entered pack ice
December 19, 1914

Trapped in pack ice
January 19, 1915

SOUTH
AMERICA

DRAKE PASSAGE

SOUTH
GEORGIA
ISLAND

WEDDELL SEA

• SOUTH POLE

ROSS SEA

ANTARCTICA

ANTARCTICA

500 MILES

THE ENDURANCE EXPEDITION, 1914-1916

△ *In January 1909, Shackleton (right) and his men trekked farther south than anyone before them, coming within 100 miles of the South Pole.*

△ *Sir Ernest Henry Shackleton.*

▽ *1914.* Endurance *on the River Thames, before departing for Antarctica.*

In the summer of 1914, a ship lay anchored in the River Thames, in London. It was called Endurance and it was being prepared for a voyage to Antarctica.

Just three years earlier, a Norwegian explorer named Roald Amundsen had been the first person to reach the South Pole. The commander of *Endurance,* Sir Ernest Henry Shackleton had tried himself to win the race for the pole, but failed. Now he was determined to set a new Antarctic record: to lead the first-ever trek across the frozen continent, from one side to the other.

Endurance was packed with gear and supplies for the voyage and the overland journey. There were dogsleds, sleeping bags and tents, guns and ammunition, compasses, maps, and tools. Piles of shining black coal were heaped on deck for the ship's engines. The hold was packed with tons of food for men and dogs, as well as books, playing cards, and scientific instruments. Shackleton expected the sea voyage to take five months, and the overland trek several more. He and his men would need to be ready for long nights and busy days.

Shackleton was already world-famous. Now his new Imperial Trans-Antarctic Expedition was the topic of newspaper stories all over England. As the crew prepared *Endurance* for the voyage, they discovered that the ship was a tourist attraction. Curious Londoners gathered on the docks to watch supplies being loaded aboard. Fans and well-wishers sent teddy bears and Bibles and good-luck charms to the crew members. Letters full of advice and prayers came flooding in from the four corners of the world.

The ship was manned by twenty-seven sailors, explorers, and scientists. One and all, they called Shackleton Boss. They believed that if anyone could lead the way across the unmapped continent, the Boss could.

On August 8, *Endurance* and its crew set sail for the frozen South.

△ *Shackleton escorts Queen Alexandra, widow of the English king Edward VI aboard* Endurance *in July 1914. The queen will inspect the ship and leave gifts for the expedition, including a Bible, a British flag, and a medal commemorating St. Christopher, patron saint of travelers.*

▷ *The original plans of* Endurance. *Built in Norway, the ship was 144 feet long and 25 feet wide. There were four decks: the bridge deck, from which the ship was steered; the main deck, containing the saloon and officers' cabins; the lower deck, containing the engine room and crew's quarters; and the hold, where coal, fresh water, and provisions were stored.*

▽ *The members of the* Endurance *expedition, photographed as the ship sailed south. Shackleton is in the center, in the hat and buttoned white sweater. Second-in-command Frank Wild is standing behind Shackleton's left shoulder. Next to Wild is the captain of* Endurance, *Frank Worsley (in the white sweater and seaman's cap).*

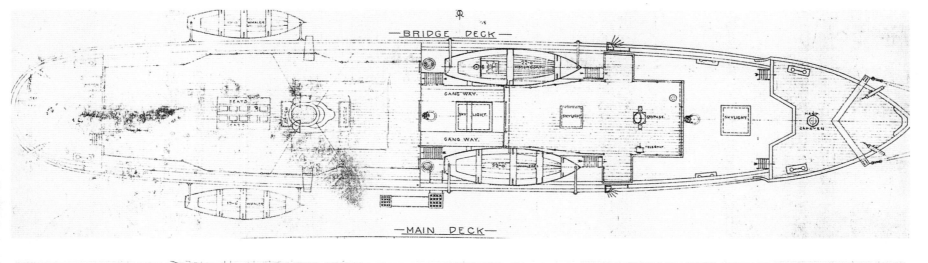

— BRIDGE DECK —

— MAIN DECK —

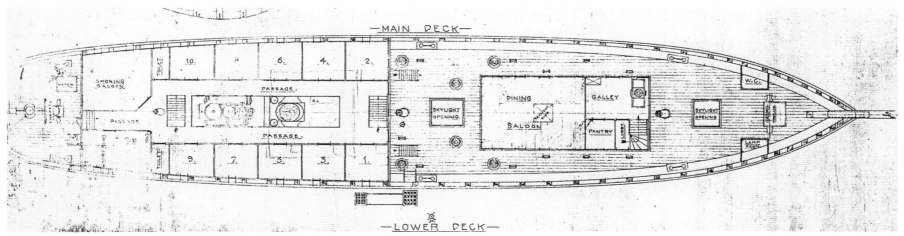

— MAIN DECK —

— LOWER DECK —

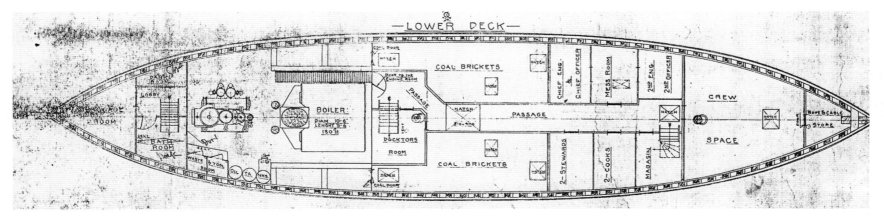

— LOWER DECK —

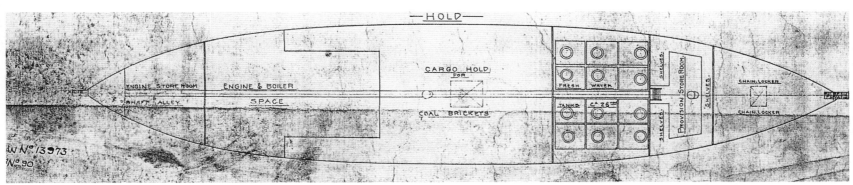

— HOLD —

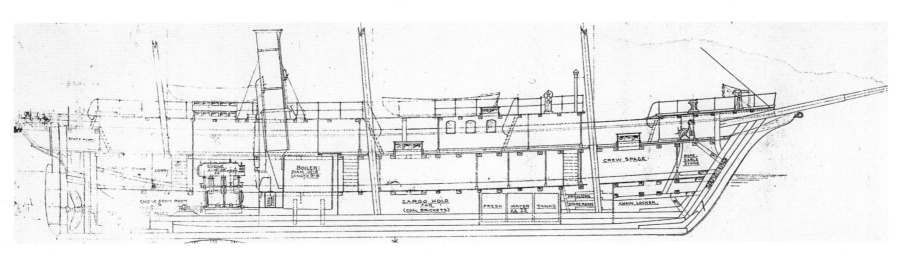

In October, *Endurance* made its first stop: Buenos Aires, Argentina. There, the crew brought on board a pack of sled dogs. The dogs were housed in kennels on both sides of the ship's deck. Mrs. Chippy, the carpenter's cat, drove the dogs wild by strolling along the tops of the kennels—just out of their reach.

There was another newcomer: a young man named Percy Blackborrow, hiding in a storage locker. When the ship was three days out from Buenos Aires, Blackborrow presented himself to the Boss.

"Do you know that on these expeditions we often get very hungry, and if there is a stowaway available he is the first to be eaten?" Shackleton warned the young adventurer fiercely.

Blackborrow boldly pointed out that Shackleton was bigger and would make a better meal. The Boss tried to hide a smile and told Blackborrow to make himself useful.

South! Endurance, *under full sail, leaves the coast of South America behind.*

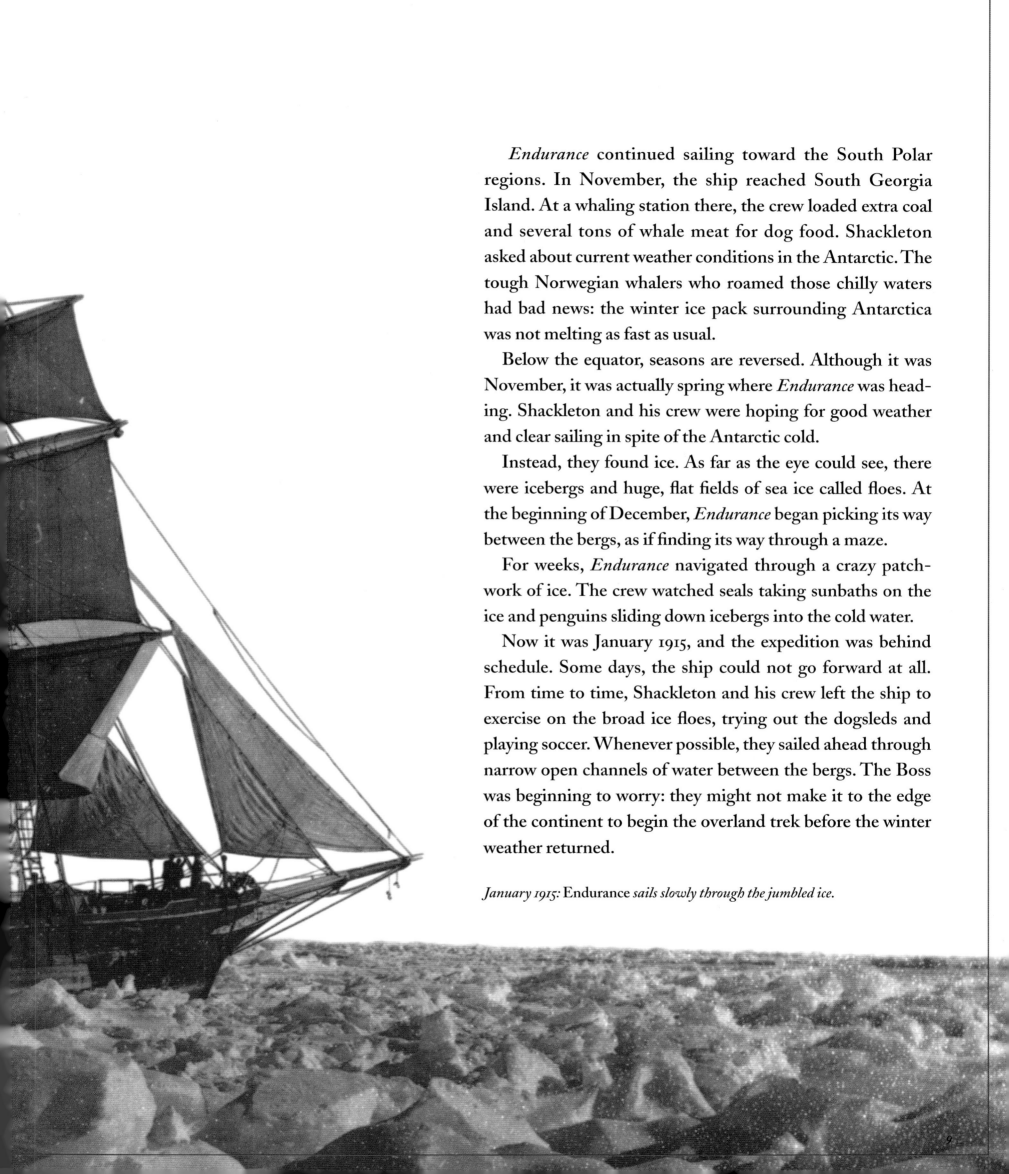

Endurance continued sailing toward the South Polar regions. In November, the ship reached South Georgia Island. At a whaling station there, the crew loaded extra coal and several tons of whale meat for dog food. Shackleton asked about current weather conditions in the Antarctic. The tough Norwegian whalers who roamed those chilly waters had bad news: the winter ice pack surrounding Antarctica was not melting as fast as usual.

Below the equator, seasons are reversed. Although it was November, it was actually spring where *Endurance* was heading. Shackleton and his crew were hoping for good weather and clear sailing in spite of the Antarctic cold.

Instead, they found ice. As far as the eye could see, there were icebergs and huge, flat fields of sea ice called floes. At the beginning of December, *Endurance* began picking its way between the bergs, as if finding its way through a maze.

For weeks, *Endurance* navigated through a crazy patchwork of ice. The crew watched seals taking sunbaths on the ice and penguins sliding down icebergs into the cold water.

Now it was January 1915, and the expedition was behind schedule. Some days, the ship could not go forward at all. From time to time, Shackleton and his crew left the ship to exercise on the broad ice floes, trying out the dogsleds and playing soccer. Whenever possible, they sailed ahead through narrow open channels of water between the bergs. The Boss was beginning to worry: they might not make it to the edge of the continent to begin the overland trek before the winter weather returned.

January 1915: Endurance *sails slowly through the jumbled ice.*

Shackleton's fears became reality on January 19, when the ice closed in around *Endurance*. The ship couldn't go forward or backward. As one crew member said, they were stuck "like an almond in the middle of a chocolate bar." As far as the men could see stretched an unbroken plain of ice.

There was nothing they could do about it. The weather was already turning colder as the short Antarctic summer came to an end. They would have to spend the winter stuck on *Endurance*.

The crew was disappointed, but they tried to make the best of things. They had plenty of food and equipment, and there were always chores to do. The scientists carried out experiments, and the sailors tended to the ship. Frank Hurley, the expedition photographer, kept himself busy taking pictures every day. Weeks stretched into months. As the ice drifted slowly through the frozen ocean, so did the ship. *Endurance* was helpless.

Six men took charge of the sled dogs. They decided to clear the kennels off the deck to give the men more room. They built "dogloos" on the ice field beside the ship and kept the dogs exercised by holding sled races. Once in a while, the dogs would spot a penguin and head after it, barking wildly. The dogsled drivers also began hunting seals. Shackleton didn't want to use up all their stored food, so they needed the seal meat—for the crew and for the dogs. They needed everything they could get to make it through the winter.

Winter at the bottom of the world. Endurance *is trapped in the Antarctic ice pack. The crew works around the ship—tending to the dogs in their ice "dogloos," cutting ice to melt into drinking water, and doing other chores. Frank Hurley, the expedition photographer, has carried his bulky box camera into the rigging to take photographs.*

As the Antarctic winter approached, the days grew shorter and shorter until there were only a few hours of sunlight each day. The men read books and played cards to keep boredom away. Every night, they gathered in the ship's common room, which they nicknamed the Ritz. They listened to records on the gramophone, played chess, and took turns reading aloud or singing—even holding "worst singer" contests. In the days before television and radio, the men were used to entertaining themselves. For a party on Midwinter's Day, June 22, they put on a variety show with costumes, silly songs, and comic skits.

The weather outside *Endurance*'s cozy cabins was terrible. Furious winds howled across the ice. Blizzards drove snow into drifts against the sides of the ship. Sometimes the wind was so fierce that it pressed the ice floes against *Endurance*. The ship's wooden timbers squeaked eerily as the pressure grew stronger. The force of the ice was so great that Shackleton began to worry that *Endurance* would be seriously damaged. What if they were forced to abandon the ship?

One night in July, at the height of a winter storm, the pressure grew stronger than ever. Shackleton shared his fears with the captain, Frank Worsley.

"If the *Endurance* does have to, well, get left behind, we will manage, somehow," Worsley said to the Boss.

Shackleton replied, "We shall hang on as long as we can. It is hard enough on the men as it is. Without a ship in which to shelter from these blizzards, and in this continuous cold—" He broke off and paced the cabin. He didn't want to think about it. But as commander of the expedition, Shackleton had to prepare for the worst.

Top: *Frank Hurley (left) and the ship's meteorologist (weatherman), Leonard Hussey, play chess during a night watch.*

Center: *Hurley's cabin on* Endurance, *which he shared with one of the expedition's two doctors, Alexander Macklin (right).*

Bottom: *Shackleton's cabin aboard* Endurance.

Opposite: Endurance *photographed at night in August 1915—the depth of the Antarctic winter. The ship is covered with frost, making it white against the inky sky.*

The ice continued to press against *Endurance* through August and September. On some days, it rammed the ship so sharply that it knocked books and tools and equipment off shelves and made the masts tremble like twigs. The men were becoming frightened and jumpy. Each time the ship let out a squeak or groan from its straining hull, they held their breath.

The crew dismantled the dogloos and brought all the animals back on board because they were afraid that the ice would break up under the dogs. One day in October, the ice pressed nonstop against the sides of *Endurance*, pushing the ship over on its port side. Everything that wasn't fastened down crashed onto the decks. For several terrifying minutes, the men thought the ship was done for.

But the pressure stopped, and *Endurance* settled back into place. They were safe—for now.

Then, in the third week of October, the pressure started up again and continued without relief. *Endurance* groaned and creaked as the ice squeezed from all sides. The timbers began to buckle and snap. Water began leaking into the hold.

The crew took turns at the pumps, trying to keep the water out, but it was no use. On October 27, Shackleton looked around at the ship, which was being crushed like a nut in a nutcracker before his eyes.

"She's going, boys. I think it's time to get off," he said.

Then the crew of *Endurance* abandoned ship—in the middle of the frozen sea.

Luckily, the destruction of *Endurance* happened in slow motion. This gave the crew plenty of time to unload food and equipment. As the ship continued to break up, the pile of gear on the ice grew larger: suitcases, books, clocks, sleeping bags, guns, crates of flour and sugar, clothes, lifeboats, diaries, axes, scrap lumber, toothbrushes, buckets—everything that could be taken off the ship was removed. The crew worked without a break. Their survival would depend on saving everything that might come in handy.

Abandon ship! Endurance *being steadily crushed by the ice. The crew members rescue everything they can: tools, provisions, sleds, lumber—and most important, the ship's three lifeboats.*

Finally, exhausted, they pitched their tents and crawled inside to sleep. Meanwhile, the timbers and rigging of *Endurance* snapped and crashed onto the deck of the dying ship.

While the rest of the men slept, Shackleton held a conference with his second-in-command, Frank Wild, and with the skipper of *Endurance,* Frank Worsley. With no way to communicate with the outside world, they were completely on their own. If they were going to survive, they would have to rescue themselves.

They came up with a plan: they would drag their three lifeboats, filled with food and equipment, across the ice to Paulet Island. It was 346 miles away. When Shackleton told the men in the morning what lay ahead of them, they reacted calmly. They trusted his leadership. If he said they would walk 346 miles, then that was what they would do.

The dogsleds, each loaded with 900 pounds of gear, went in the lead. The drivers struggled to hack a path through the jumbled ice field with axes and shovels. Behind came the three boats, pulled in stages by fifteen men in harness. They dragged one boat forward a quarter of a mile, left it, and returned for the second boat. When the third boat was hauled up to join the other two, they began dragging the first boat again.

But it was torture. The surface of the ice was broken and uneven, and the men sometimes sank to their knees in freezing slush while snow swirled down onto them. After two hours of backbreaking labor, they were only a mile from *Endurance.* At this rate, they would never reach Paulet Island. The floe they were on was solid: they would set up camp and stay put.

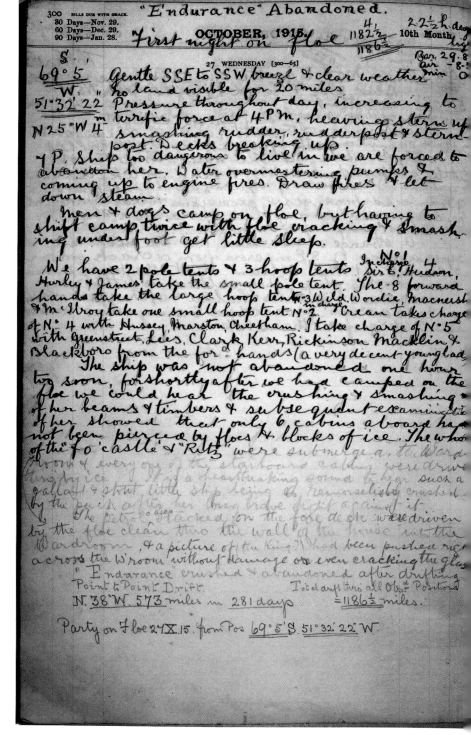

△ *Captain Frank Worsley's logbook describes the day* Endurance *was abandoned. "The ship was not abandoned one hour too soon, for shortly after we had camped on the floe we could hear the crushing and smashing up of her beams and timbers. . . ."*

▽ *Dragging one of* Endurance's *lifeboats across the ice.*

△ *This photograph was taken the morning after the crew abandoned ship. Tents and piles of supplies are scattered on the ice while* Endurance *lies partly crushed in the background. The men called this site "Dump Camp."*

Ocean Camp. There are five tents for sleeping and a storage tent, made from lumber and canvas salvaged from Endurance. The galley (kitchen) has a stove made from pieces of Endurance's boiler and is sheltered by walls made from one of the ship's sails. The expedition's crew is kept busy hunting on sled and skis, mending the boats, and doing other chores.

Ocean Camp was to be their home for the next two months. They returned to *Endurance* for more equipment and food. With lumber rescued from the ship, they built a cookhouse to hold an oil stove.

Then they settled in to wait. Shackleton knew that the ice they were camped on was drifting north and would carry them to the open ocean. Eventually, they would need to take to the lifeboats. Once the ice drifted into warmer waters, it would not be stable enough to camp on. Their only hope of rescue lay across the water. So the carpenter worked on improving the boats and making them more seaworthy.

The Antarctic spring was under way now, and temperatures sometimes climbed into the thirties, which seemed almost tropical to the men. They continued to hunt, to exercise the dogs, and to keep themselves busy with books and card games and chores. Just keeping their gear dry in slushy Ocean Camp was a steady job.

Slowly, the ice drifted away from Antarctica. Large cracks appeared on their ice floe. The surface became soft. November 21 brought an unforgettable event: the broken, twisted wreck of *Endurance* finally slipped through the ice and sank forever. In December, Shackleton decided they should move again, hoping to narrow the distance between themselves and Paulet Island.

But the going was tough: it still took three days to cover seven miles. After two more days of backbreaking effort, it looked as though they were stuck. The ice was mushy and unstable. They couldn't go back. They couldn't go forward. They would have to make another camp.

They called this one Patience Camp, and patience was what they needed. The year 1915 was drawing to a close and the new year was before them.

What lay ahead? Shackleton couldn't be sure. The drift of the ice was haphazard. Sometimes they were carried north, sometimes east or west.

The months of February and March dragged by. Sadly, the Boss decided it was time for the dogs to be killed. There would be no way to save them once the boats were launched. One by one, they were led away and destroyed with a quick, merciful shot to the head.

By early April, the ice floe that Patience Camp sat on was alarmingly small, and leads of open sea surrounded them. Killer whales spouted in the water as they hunted seals. The men could feel the rise and fall of the ocean lifting their floe, and some of them began to feel seasick.

On April 8, Shackleton gave the order: "Launch the boats!"

Thousands of birds circled overhead as the crew shoved the boats off the ice. Sitting on their gear and their last crates of food, the men bent to the oars. Waves crashed against icebergs. The three boats picked their way through the maze of ice, pulling north toward the open ocean.

As the light faded, they began looking out for an ice floe to camp on. Shackleton soon spotted one. Luckily, a large seal was sleeping on it, and the men quickly killed it and cooked it for dinner. Then they pitched their tents and tried to get some rest.

The next days were filled with danger and hard work. Once they left the shelter of the ice pack, the violence of the open ocean met them like a hurricane. Waves broke over the tiny, crowded lifeboats, and howling winds and sleet lashed the men's faces. The temperature sank. The men could hear ice crackling on their clothes and on the sails that now filled with wind. Sleep was out of the question. They were low on drinking water and short on food. The men were beginning to break.

Shackleton feared that the boats would become separated or that some of the men would die of exhaustion. But ahead of them, somewhere, lay a tiny, rocky islet called Elephant Island. If they could make that, they would be able to rest.

At the limit of their strength, the men saw Elephant Island between tattered rags of mist. They had been in the boats for seven days, climbing giant waves, trying to keep from freezing—seven days with little sleep, little food, no water. When at last they landed, the men fell to their knees on the shore, weeping and laughing.

It was the first time in almost a year and a half that they had stood on solid ground.

Launch the boats! The crew, with their provisions, crowd into three small lifeboats—the James Caird, *the* Dudley Docker, *and the* Stancomb Wills—*and set out for Elephant Island, 100 miles away across a stormy sea littered with icebergs.*

Elephant Island was solid ground, but it was also uninhabited, and winter was approaching. They could not just wait for a ship to come along and rescue them—it might never happen.

After three days of much-needed rest, Shackleton announced that he would take the best boat, the *James Caird*, and sail back to South Georgia Island, over 800 miles away, to get help. He would take Captain Worsley, for his sailing skills; the carpenter, Harry McNeish, in case the boat needed repairs on the way; and three other men. After he reached the whaling station, he would return to rescue the crew.

McNeish reinforced the boat. The men collected fresh water from a glacier on the island. They made the *James Caird* as seaworthy as possible. On April 24, 1916, the *James Caird* shoved off.

For more than two weeks, Shackleton and his five-man crew sailed across the stormiest ocean in the world, facing 100-foot waves, bitter temperatures, and hurricane-force winds. The twenty-two-foot boat was often covered with ice, and the men had to crawl across the decking while the boat heaved and pitched to chop the ice away.

They slept in shifts, crawling into the bow to grab what rest they could. Worsley navigated the best he knew how, although conditions were terrible. In order to calculate their position, he had to be able to see the sun at noon—and with the stormy weather, that was possible only four times. If they lost their way and missed South Georgia Island, they would be headed out into the vast Atlantic Ocean, and that would mean certain death. The men were constantly drenched with salt water and spray as waves broke across the boat. They ached with cold.

Shackleton kept them going with hot meals and drinks—six times a day. Lighting their little camp stove on the bucking boat was tricky, and the moment their cocoa or stew was ready, they put the stove out to save fuel. They learned to eat and drink their meals scalding hot and let the food warm their numbed bodies.

If Shackleton feared they wouldn't make it, he never let on. Day after day he sat at the tiller, scanning the horizon. And with Worsley's almost miraculous skill with compass and sextant, the battered boat and its exhausted crew reached the island on the seventeenth day.

The voyage of the James Caird. *Only twenty-two feet long, the boat has two masts and three small sails and is steered by a rope yoke attached to the rudder. Worsley calculates the* Caird's *position by sighting the sun through an instrument called a sextant. The cutaway shows the cramped space below, where one man sleeps in the bow and two prepare a meal using a camp stove.*

There was just one problem: they had landed on the southwest side of the island, and the whaling station was on the northeast side. The boat was too damaged to risk sailing it around in the stormy waters. But the interior of the island was blocked by a range of jagged mountains and glaciers. They would have to cross it on foot.

Two of the men were completely broken down and a third would have to stay and look after them. That left Shackleton, Worsley, and second officer Tom Crean to make the hike across South Georgia Island.

Their mountaineering equipment wasn't the best gear they could have wished for on a climb such as this one. They had an ax and fifty feet of rope. They studded the soles of their boots with nails for a better grip on the icy peaks. They rested for several days. Then, with food for three days and a small camping stove, they set out, crossing the first snowfield by moonlight.

Months of poor nutrition and inactivity had left them in no shape for a rugged hike. But as the Boss said long afterward, "The thought of those fellows on Elephant Island kept us going all the time….If you're a leader, a fellow that other fellows look to, you've got to keep going. That was the thought which sailed us through the hurricane and tugged us up and down those mountains."

South Georgia Island had never been crossed before. There were no trails, no clue which passes led to safety and which ones led to sheer drops. The men rested and cooked quick meals, and pushed on. The Boss didn't dare let them stop to sleep, fearing that they might lose the will to continue. On they trudged, hour after hour, through the first night and a day, then another night. By the next morning, they were haggard, exhausted, and trembling with cold, but they were within sight of the eastern coast.

Faintly, from far below, came the sound of the seven o'clock whistle at the whaling station. They had reached safety at last.

After more than a year trapped in the ice, an 800-mile open-boat journey, and a two-day trek over uncharted mountains, Shackleton, Worsley, and Crean approach a whaling station on South Georgia Island, only minutes from safety.

Back on Elephant Island, the rest of the crew had no idea of the Boss's triumph. Once the *James Caird* had disappeared from view, the twenty-two remaining members of the expedition set to work. Frank Wild, in charge, decided on the first task. Antarctic winter was sweeping up from the South Pole, and they would have to shelter themselves from it.

They scavenged the beach for rocks and built a low foundation. Then they took the two remaining boats, the *Dudley Docker* and the *Stancomb Wills,* and turned them upside down over the stones. The tattered canvas sails were lashed across the boats, and the chinks in the walls were stuffed with moss to keep out the wind. They rigged a chimney from some small sheets of metal and installed the blubber stove. When they were done, they had a crude hut to wait out the winter in.

The first storms came quickly. While the winds howled outside their cabin, the men kept each other company. A popular pastime was listing their favorite foods—after a steady diet of seal meat and penguin, the men dreamed of fresh fruit, cakes, and roast beef. The hours passed slowly. The days passed slowly. The weeks passed slowly. Camp Wild was a dreary place.

There were jobs to do: ice had to be chipped off the glaciers and melted for drinking water. There were penguins and seals to hunt.

And there was an operation to be performed. Percy Blackborrow's feet had frozen on the boat journey to Elephant Island, and gangrene had set in. Now the toes on his left foot were dead and black and had to be amputated. There were few medical supplies left. But the expedition's doctors, James McIlroy and Alexander Macklin, performed the surgery by the light of a seal oil lamp.

Outside the hut, the winds screamed over the cliffs of Elephant Island. Sea ice crowded the shore. They knew Shackleton could not return until the winter was over.

Wild tried to keep the men optimistic. Every morning, he rolled up his sleeping bag and said to the men, "Get your things ready, boys. The Boss may come today."

But as the months went by, they began to wonder if "today" would ever come.

Camp Wild. The Dudley Docker *and the* Stancomb Wills *have been overturned and covered with sails to make a hut, where the remaining members of the crew wait for Shackleton to return with a rescue ship.*

When Shackleton, Worsley, and Crean walked into the whaling station on May 20, they looked like wild men. They were in rags, their faces black from oily smoke, and their hair and beards long and matted. Dogs barked in alarm as they staggered to the station manager's house.

"Who the devil are you?" asked the manager.

"My name is Shackleton," the Boss replied.

There was stunned silence. No one had expected to see Shackleton alive, let alone see him come walking down from the peaks of South Georgia Island. But when the Boss told their story, they were treated as heroes.

The three weary men were given hot baths and hot food, and allowed to sleep. As soon as they awoke, Shackleton began arranging a rescue party. Worsley set out in a boat with some of the whalers to pick up the men on the other side of the island.

A steamer was outfitted to make for Elephant Island, and Shackleton left at once. But the weather and the ocean were against him. He was forced to turn back for South Georgia Island. Twice more he tried, but the cruel Antarctic winter was too brutal.

June and July went by, and Shackleton was desperate to get his men. At last, in August, he took a Chilean ship called the *Yelcho* and made once more for Elephant Island.

On August 30, George Marston, the expedition artist, was keeping lookout at Camp Wild. On the horizon, he saw the smoke of a ship's funnel. "SHIP HO!" he yelled.

The *Yelcho* steamed into the bay, and a boat was lowered over the side. It was Shackleton. "Are all well?" he shouted as soon as he was near enough.

"YES!"

The men crowded around the Boss as he landed, shaking his hand. "We knew you'd come back," one said to him.

They had all survived. Shackleton had returned to take them home.

Rescue! Shackleton returns to Elephant Island to bring home his men. In the background is the Yelcho, *the ship that Shackleton borrowed from the Chilean government for the rescue attempt.*

World War I was raging in Europe when the men arrived home. But news of their amazing journey made headlines around the world in spite of the war. Most of the members of the expedition immediately joined in the fighting. Shackleton himself led a command in northern Russia, with some of his companions from *Endurance* serving under him.

At the war's end, Shackleton turned his sights toward the Antarctic again. He could not get exploring out of his blood. His health had suffered permanently from the hardships of his last trip, but he sailed south in late 1921.

By January 1922, he reached South Georgia Island, but he was near the end of his endurance. He suffered a heart attack on board his ship.

As Shackleton lay in bed dying, Dr. Macklin tried to ease his pain. "You'll have to change your way of life, Boss," his old friend said.

But the Boss would never give up his goal. He died in South Georgia Island and was buried there.

It wasn't until decades later that anyone crossed the continent of Antarctica. Sir Edmund Hillary, famous for making the first ascent of Mt. Everest, led an expedition that passed the South Pole on January 4, 1958, and continued onward to the other side. Instead of dogsleds, he used motorized tractor-sleds.

No traces remained of Shackleton's camps, of course. They had long since been swallowed by the ice. But the Boss's spirit survives in the Antarctic. It is the spirit of *Endurance*.

△ *Monument to Shackleton on South Georgia Island. The inscription reads, "Sir Ernest Shackleton, Explorer. Died here January 5, 1922. Erected by his comrades."*

▽ *Members of the* Endurance *expedition photographed in Chile after their rescue. The man in uniform is the captain of the* Yelcho. *To his right are Shackleton (in the hat), Wild, Worsley (in the cap), and Crean (smiling).*

February 15, 1874: Ernest Henry Shackleton born in County Kildare, Ireland

January 9, 1909: Shackleton leads an expedition within 100 miles of the South Pole

August 8, 1914: *Endurance* departs from England

October 26: *Endurance* departs from Buenos Aires, Argentina

December 5: *Endurance* departs from South Georgia Island

December 19: *Endurance* enters the Antarctic ice pack

December 31: *Endurance* crosses the Antarctic Circle

January 19, 1915: *Endurance* trapped by ice

October 27: *Endurance* abandoned

October 31 to December 23: Ocean Camp

November 21: *Endurance* sinks

December 28 to April 8: Patience Camp

April 8, 1916: Boats launched

April 15: Landing on Elephant Island

April 24: *James Caird* departs from Elephant Island

May 10: *James Caird* lands on South Georgia Island

May 20: Shackleton, Worsley, and Crean reach Stromness whaling station

August 30: Shackleton returns to Elephant Island aboard the *Yelcho*

January 5, 1922: Shackleton dies on South Georgia Island

MEMBERS OF THE IMPERIAL TRANS-ANTARCTIC EXPEDITION

Sir Ernest Shackleton *Leader*

Frank Wild *Second-in-Command*

Frank Worsley *Captain of* Endurance

Hubert Hudson *Navigating Officer*

Lionel Greenstreet *First Officer*

Thomas Crean *Second Officer*

Alfred Cheetham *Third Officer*

Louis Rickinson *Chief Engineer*

A. J. Kerr *Second Engineer*

Dr. James McIlroy *Surgeon*

Dr. Alexander Macklin *Surgeon*

Robert Clark *Biologist*

Leonard Hussey *Meteorologist*

James Wordie *Geologist*

Reginald James *Physicist*

George Marston *Artist*

Thomas Orde-Lees *Motor Expert*

Frank Hurley *Photographer*

Harry McNeish *Carpenter*

Charles Green *Cook*

Percy Blackborrow *Steward*

John Vincent *Able Seaman*

Timothy McCarthy *Able Seaman*

Walter How *Able Seaman*

William Bakewell *Able Seaman*

Thomas McLeod *Able Seaman*

William Stevenson *Fireman*

Ernest Holness *Fireman*

RESOURCE GUIDE

BOOKS FOR CHILDREN

Jennifer Armstrong, *Shipwreck at the Bottom of the World*. An account of the *Endurance* expedition for older readers by the author of this book.

Michael McCurdy, *Trapped by the Ice*. A picture book for younger readers.

BOOKS FOR ADULTS

Caroline Alexander, *The Endurance: Shackleton's Legendary Antarctic Expedition*. Contains most of Frank Hurley's original pictures from the expedition.

Ernest H. Shackleton, *South*. Shackleton's own account of the *Endurance* expedition.

Frank A. Worsley, *Shackleton's Boat Journey*. Captain Frank Worsley's account of the expedition describes the boat journey from Elephant Island to South Georgia Island in detail.

VIDEO

South: Ernest Shackleton and the Endurance Expedition. Frank Hurley's silent movie recording the expedition.

INDEX

Text copyright © 2000 by Jennifer M. Armstrong
Illustrations copyright © 2000 by William Maughan

All rights reserved. No part of this book may be reproduced or transmitted in any form or by any means, electronic or mechanical, including photocopying, recording, or by any information storage and retrieval system, without permission in writing from the publisher.

Published by Crown Publishers, a division of Random House, Inc., 1540 Broadway, New York, New York 10036.

CROWN and colophon are trademarks of Random House, Inc.

www.randomhouse.com/kids

Photograph on page 17 courtesy of the Royal Geographic Society. All other photographs courtesy of the Scott Polar Research Institute.

Plans of *Endurance* on page 5 courtesy of the National Maritime Museum, Greenwich, England.

Map by Kailey LeFaiver

Library of Congress Cataloging-in-Publication Data
Armstrong, Jennifer, 1961–
Spirit of Endurance / Jennifer Armstrong ; illustrated by William Maughan. — 1st ed.
p.   cm.
1. Shackleton, Ernest Henry, Sir, 1874–1922—Journeys. 2. Endurance (Ship). 3. Imperial Trans-Antarctic Expedition (1914–1916).
4. Antarctica—Discovery and exploration. I. Title.
G850 1914 .S53A767 2000
919.8'904—dc21   99-37450

ISBN 0-517-80091-8 (trade)—0-517-80092-6 (lib. bdg.)

Printed in Hong Kong
September 2000
10 9 8 7 6 5 4 3 2 1
First Edition